CW01657825

UNBELIEVABLE STORIES OF MICHAEL JORDAN

THIS BOOK BELONGS TO:

UNBELIEVABLE STORIES OF
MICHAEL JORDAN

INTRODUCTION

Michael Jordan is a household name when it comes to basketball. He is famous for his competitive nature, high self-discipline, and magnificent moves on the court.

Michael led his team, the Chicago Bulls, to six NBA championships. He also received the NBA Most Valuable Player (MVP) Award five times in his life!

Michael was born on February 17, 1963. His mother, Delores, was a bank teller. His father, James, worked in maintenance but later became the manager at General Electrics. Michael has four other siblings.

Michael attended university at North Carolina, where he also played for the team. Shortly after, in 1984, he began playing basketball professionally. He proved himself to be a skillful player, with a marvelous record of triumphs. But he was not without some setbacks. Life has not been easy for Michael, but he has never let life events dictate his life destiny. He continues to tread uncharted, and often risky waters.

Chapter 1:

His Brother as His First Opponent

When Michael was a few years old, his father took him outside to their backyard. Michael saw a long, thin stick and a small white ball. "This, son, is called a bat. And here is the ball," Michael's father, James, explained.

Michael looked, eyes wide, and tried to lift the bat. His small fingers could barely wrap around the handle. He noticed that his father was putting on a big brown glove. "With this, we catch the ball."

After that day, Michael and his father played baseball every day. James was a patient man, taking his time to help his young son learn the basics of the game.

When Michael was a little older, his older brother Larry, came home one day with a big orange ball under his arm. Michael followed Larry outside, where he started shooting the ball into the basketball hoop. The sight of his older brother dribbling the ball, leaping into the air, and aiming for the hoop mesmerized the young Michael. He wanted to be able to hold, dribble, and shoot that big ball just like his brother.

When Michael asked Larry to teach him how to play, Larry agreed. He felt secretly happy about his little brother's request. If Michael learned to play basketball, Larry would have an opponent at home. They could practice together all the time. Young Michael listened to his brother's instructions with eyes and ears wide open. He wanted to learn as quickly as possible. And he did!

Even though he learned quickly and knew how to play, Michael lost many games to Larry. Like many boys his age, Michael hated losing. He resolved to practice and work hard until he could beat his older brother every time. He got up extra early to practice, he played at school during recess, and soon, Michael won every game against his older brother. Larry had helped Michael unleash his competitive nature. Michael had a taste of sweet victory! His desire to keep winning gave him the motivation to push himself to work hard.

Chapter 2:

Fear of Water

It is easy to think that Michael is fearless. His movements on the court are swift and graceful. But, few people know Michael's deepest fear: water.

On a sizzling summer day, young Michael and his friend went out to swim in a nearby lake. Shortly after the friends had jumped into the water, Michael saw his friend's arms waving in and out of the water as he shouted for help. Before Michael could do anything, his friend was pulled down by an undercurrent and drowned. This was an incredibly sad and life-changing experience for a young child.

A few years later, Michael was at a baseball camp. It was another scorching summer day. All the children in the camp were going to swim in a river to cool off. Michael was nervous, remembering his last tragic experience, but he told himself to be brave and to face his fears. Being brave is not about the lack of fear, but trying even when you are afraid. Michael showed his bravery again, by trying to swim. However, he started to panic and almost drowned from moving too fast and forgetting to breathe.

This was his second terrible experience with water. He had almost drowned. How did Michael respond to these bad experiences? Did they make Michael scared and timid? No—quite the opposite. Michael focused on his strengths and became a great champion. He focused on what he wanted to achieve and worked hard on it. To this day, Michael admits to being uncomfortable near water. He learned not to let his fear affect other parts of his life or to let it stop him from practicing hard and believing in himself. His confidence was unshaken.

t

Chapter 3:

Cut from the High School Team

As a high school student, Michael desperately wanted to join the basketball team at his school. He wasn't the only one! A lot of other kids wanted to get on the team too, but not everyone could join. Kids had to be picked by the coaches.

Even though Michael was tall, especially for a fifteen year old boy, there were older boys taller than him. It helps to be tall in basketball, but you need other skills too.

Michael practiced day and night, whenever he had free time outside of school and house chores. Finally, the day to try out for the team arrived. Many high school boys gathered in the gym, each waiting nervously to be called upon by the coach. When Michael's turn came, he walked confidently towards the hoop. He dribbled and performed a perfect shot. The coaches looked pleased. Michael was sure he would get in.

The next day the results came out. Michael stood among the many other young boys eager to see their name on the team members name page. Michael looked up and down the list many times. But his name was not there.

Michael was not selected. He was not part of the team. The coaches had chosen other boys, older, taller, and stronger than him. Michael felt crushed, the losing feeling he hated so much washed over him. However, Michael used those sad feelings to push himself even further. When most people might have given up, he didn't. Michael was not most people.

Michael asked the coach if he could go with the team to their first game. Seeing the determination in young Michael, the coach agreed. He asked Michael to carry the jerseys and equipment for the other players. Michael was disappointed that he wouldn't get to play, but he did what the coach asked anyway. He did not let anything get in his way of playing the game he loved.

Chapter 4:

Accidental Best Friend

Michael was twenty-one years old when the Chicago Bulls drafted him. The manager of the team sent Michael an airplane ticket and flew him down to Chicago. Michael got on the airplane, a suitcase in his hand and big dreams in his heart. He was talented, but he also had learned the value of challenging work.

Now he was ready to test himself in the NBA. Another important quality Michael has is open-mindedness. That means that he tries to not judge people and is open to new experiences. And this was certainly going to be a new experience.

Michael's plane eventually landed in Chicago. It was midnight. Michael's seat was all the way in the back of the airplane, which meant he was one of the last people to get off the airplane. When he finally walked down the stairs from the airplane, there was hardly anybody left at the airport. Most people had already left, and a few stragglers were passing by. At that time, nobody knew Michael, so no cameras followed him. But he had expected the managers to send him a driver to take him back to the hotel. But there was no driver sent. Michael had no idea how to get to his destination, especially that late at night.

Michael looked around uncomfortably. He noticed another man, his eyes searching the airport as if he were waiting for someone. After a few minutes, the man approached Michael. He asked if Michael needed a driver. Michael said yes! It was a delightful coincidence. The man said that his customer never came, so he is free to take Michael anywhere. The driver was George Koehler. George gave Michael a tour of the city and eventually dropped him off at his hotel. The two stayed in touch and eventually Michael hired George as his personal assistant, but their relationship was stronger than that. Michael said George was his best friend. Michael had an open mind and, because of his openness, he was able to find a life-long friend in George.

Chapter 5:

Injured During His Second NBA Season

A twenty-two-year-old Michael was now gearing up for the upcoming NBA season. His renowned will and competitiveness meant he was always practicing. All that practice had sharpened his skills, but unfortunately, after pushing himself so hard, Michael broke his foot! He arrived for new basketball season, but his foot was not completely healed. He was still in pain. But for Michael, pain was not important. He was completely certain that he would play the game no matter what.

You can imagine Michael's frustration when his team doctor told him that he couldn't play. The doctor explained that his foot had not healed properly. He also told Michael that if he played, there was a small chance that his foot injury would become so bad that it would end his basketball career.

Michael's career had just started. This was a significant risk to take. But for Michael, the decision was clear. He insisted that he would play, despite that risk. When the doctor saw his persistence, he called a meeting with Michael's coach, in the hopes of convincing the young star to come to his senses.

As always, Michael was determined. He had made up his mind and nothing, not even a career-ending risk, would change it. His coach tried to explain the situation to Michael.

"If you have a bad headache and the doctor says, here is a bottle of pills. There are ten pills in it. Nine will help with your headache but there is one pill that would kill you. Would you take the pill?" the coach asked him.

"It depends on how bad the headache is," Michael replied.

Michael played the game, ignoring his pain and the risk to his career. He persevered, or stuck with it, through every game; helping his team win the championship that year.

BULLS
91
BULLS
33
BULLS
23
BULLS
9
BULLS
7

Chapter 6:

Jordan Rules

In 1988, a team called the Detroit Pistons produced a plan for trying to beat Michael Jordan and the Bulls. He was legendary on the court, but this team found a way to throw Michael off his game. They called their strategy "Jordan Rules." Their rules were all about not letting Michael get to the basket or forcing him to change his direction. Then another player would run full force at Michael and hit himself against Michael's body.

As a result of this, Michael's team lost repeatedly to the Pistons. At the end of that season, Michael was mentally, physically, and emotionally drained. He had been literally knocked down time after time. After losing seven games to them, Michael decided it was time to change. He worked hard to improve his skill of catching the ball near the hoop. That way, he did not need to dribble up and be knocked down by other big players.

13
BULLS
23

It worked! Michael was once again undefeatable. He was the master of the game and could overcome any obstacles as he desired. Even though he was tired and had lost those seven games, he did not let that stop him. He found a way to beat his opponents at their own game and once again won the championship.

BULLS
23

Chapter 7:

The Stolen Jersey

By 1990, Michael Jordan was famous, known for his high jumps and dunk shots. He also became known for doing certain things before every game, such as eating a large meal of steak and potatoes. Michael also always made sure that his jersey number was 23. That's why, even today, the number 23 reminds people of Michael Jordan.

During a game in 1990, Michael was getting ready to go out and onto the court. His teammates had already put on their jerseys, but Michael's jersey was missing. He searched his locker and the room, but nothing. A frantic search ensued, with everybody searching everywhere for the number 23 jersey. But no matter how hard they tried, no one could find that jersey. The clock was ticking, the game would start any minute!

BULLS
12

His manager brought a nameless jersey, numbered twelve. He handed the jersey to Michael. Michael had always worn number 23. Was this a bad sign? Michael thought about it and eventually accepted the jersey, pulling it over his head. The game started promptly. If Michael was going to give a stellar performance, he needed to get over the shock and frustration of his stolen jersey. Michael didn't let his feelings or questions of what happened to his jersey throw him off his game. He bounced back and dominated the basketball court in his nameless jersey.

No one needed to see Michael's name printed on his back. His awe-inspiring skills were all anyone needed to spot Michael among the crowd of players. Michael went on to score forty-eight points during that game.

Chapter 8:

The Tragic Death of His Father

One day, in North Carolina, in Michael's hometown, two teenage boys decided to rob a car. They had guns. They found a car that they liked and got ready to steal it. The owner of that car was James Jordan, Michael's father.

That day, James was tired. He decided to take a little nap in his car to regain his energy. He sat behind the steering wheel and closed his eyes. Suddenly he heard a clicking noise as his front door opened. His eyes shot open, widened with fear and shock. The two teenage boys saw James after they managed to unlock the car door. One of them panicked and fired his gun. James Jordan died that day, July 23, 1993.

The news of his father's tragic death broke Michael's heart. He had loved his father so much. He called his father, "the voice of reason" and the one who "always drove me and challenged me." His father was Michael's rock. They were very close and his father always gave him great life advice.

Now his dear father was no longer alive. It changed his life to lose his father. But, in that time of difficulty, Michael remembered his father words that reminded him to always turn a negative into a positive.

What do people usually do when a family member dies? It is painful to lose someone you love, especially a family member. Sometimes people become angry or sad, or don't want to be around other people because their hearts hurt so much from the loss.

Michael was sad, too, but wanted to honor the memory of his father, by switching from basketball to baseball. He had played baseball many times with his father. His father had encouraged Michael to play baseball professionally.

So now, with his father gone, Michael overcame his sadness and took action to become an even better athlete.

Chapter 9:

Chicago Bulls Eliminated

In 1995, Michael and his team, the Chicago Bulls, were getting ready to compete in the soon-to-be famous NBA playoffs coming up. They had practiced hard and had to win against other teams in the playoffs to advance. The Chicago Bulls won their first few games in the playoffs. But despite this, the Bulls lost to a team called the Orlando Magic. This loss would mean the end of playing basketball for the season, they did not get to move forward and play in the championship. The team was eliminated from the playoffs.

BULLS

The worst part was that it was a shot that Michael missed during the last few minutes of the game, that might have been what cost the team the game. If Michael had made that basket, the team would have qualified to advance. Michael was disappointed with himself. His team had lost. Michael felt that he had let his teammates down. He was full of sad and upset feelings. But as you can imagine, Michael did not let this become an obstacle.

The very next day, Michael decided to practice harder and with more focus than he ever had in his life. And we know that he had already practiced a lot! Michael felt the pride that comes with winning in a game. He wouldn't let anything take that feeling away. He worked hard, through pain, knee injury, a broken foot, and sore muscles and improved his game. The next year, his team played against the Orlando Magic again. This time, Michael was prepared. They had an amazing victory and swept the series 4-0. He had worked tirelessly for the entire year and now he was a winner again.

Chapter 10:

The Bad Pizza Game

The night before one of the last games of the 1997 NBA Finals, Michael and his team were both excited and nervous. This was the game that would make them champions if they won. The team was staying at a hotel and decided to order some food. But it was late. The hotel food delivery service had already closed. A team member suggested that they order pizza. Everyone agreed and before long, the aroma of pepperoni, cheese and tomato sauce had filled the room where Michael and his teammates were. When the pizza arrived, the team members were surprised to see that five delivery guys had come! They all were carrying pizzas. The basketball players got suspicious and started to doubt. Why did five men come to deliver pizza? Something wasn't right.

BULLS

Michael was the only one who ate that pizza. Everyone else was too suspicious and refused.

Around 2 am, Michael's roommate woke up from a whimpering noise. He turned on the lamp, looked down and saw Michael crouched on the floor. Michael was shaking and moaning from pain. His roommate instantly called the coach.

It turned out that the pizza was indeed bad. It was now only hours before the game. Michael was in pain. Everyone wondered if Michael would stay out of this game. But to everyone's surprise, he told everyone that he would still play. They tried to persuade him to just rest. After all this was just one game. There would always be other chances. But Michael, whose determination and will-power knew no bounds, refused to listen to them.

BULLS
23

During the game, Michael used all his will power to focus on the game and ignore his body that was in obvious pain. His muscles were shaking, his eyesight blurry. Despite all this, Michael persisted the entire game. He kept on making every possible effort to bring his best game on for his team. Michael did not just settle for average effort. He gave his best to the game. The Chicago Bulls went on to win the NBA championship that year.

That's Michael Jordan.

THE END

Printed in Great Britain
by Amazon

22043651R00046